ENTER WATER, SWIMMER

Praise for Enter Water, Swimmer

"Mary Morris's debut collection unleashes the forces of Eros against those of Thanatos—love and all that is sustaining versus utter annihilation. You can sense Frida Kahlo as the presiding spirit here; the poems arrive with totemic intensity, a surreal mash-up of animism, mysticism, cultural traditions, and harrowing autobiography—all in the service of a spirit seeking remedy for a vulnerable body in a hazardous world. As in Coltrane's 'A Love Supreme,' the work here is psalm-like, exultant, a blooming outward from suffering via the 'blue throat of joy.'"

—Thomas Centolella, winner of the American Book Award

"A distinguished collection, written with style and confidence. The poet continually introduces elements that surprise. The collection as a whole speaks with authority."

—X.J. Kennedy, winner of the Poetry Society of America's Robert Frost Medal for lifetime service to poetry

ENTER WATER,
SWIMMER

*For Kaz, who keeps me
moving in the morning!
Much Love,*

Mary Morris

Mary Morris 2018

Texas Review Press
Huntsville, Texas

FIRST EDITION

Requests for permission to acknowledge material from the work should be sent to:

Permissions
Texas Review Press
English Department
Sam Houston State University
Huntsville, TX 77341-2146

Cover photo: "Zanzibar" by Mary Morris

Cover design: Nancy Parsons, www.graphicdesigngroup.net

Author photo: Ken Apt

Library of Congress Cataloging-in-Publication Data

Names: Morris, Mary, 1953- eauthor.
Title: Enter water, swimmer / Mary Morris.
Description: First edition. | Huntsville, Texas : Texas Review Press, [2018]
    | Includes bibliographical references. |
Identifiers: LCCN 2018002043 (print) | LCCN 2018004160 (ebook) | ISBN
    9781680031553 (ebook) | ISBN 9781680031546 | ISBN 9781680031546¬(pbk.)
Subjects: LCSH: Women--Poetry. | Femininity--Poetry.
Classification: LCC PS3613.O7739 (ebook) | LCC PS3613.O7739 A6 2018 (print) |
    DDC 811/.6--dc23

LC record available at https://lccn.loc.gov/2018002043

for Daniel and Ken

Contents

II

ENTER WATER,
SWIMMER

Leave the Barren Fields

Enter water, swimmer.
Touch the muddy floor.

Reappear dripping
to be born for this.

Cover the body with honey
on the night of a new moon.

Gather your voice at the river,
sing with the loon.

Awaken at midnight feedings.
Draw the body.

Paint in panthers,
ruby-lit flowers.

Read Grimm's fairy tales
to children in the next village.

Adopt a field or a horse.
Take on a juvenile

stealing your money for her affliction
or a boy herding his bony cow

across Darfur.
Be sworn in.

Hymn

Horses drink the night
from Jade Lake mirrored with stars.

All thirst, they draw water
behind their chess-piece teeth.

Once, we swam Appaloosas
across the Milky Way of rivers.

At fifteen, your brother inhaled
vapors of carbon monoxide.

In 1969 the word was *fag*.
Wherever you are, speak to others

kneeling in pastures green as Lorca's.
Protect them from executioners,

the tilted crown leading a swarm.

Cerebral Hemorrhage, Five Months with Child, Christmas Eve

The head was boiling with bees.
    The wound, futile. Your small hand

appeared as sound. We listened.
    It was the darkened month—
season without apples.

I thought I fell asleep in your dreams—
    a three day coma:

a wolf's eyes flecked with mirrors.
    Its jaw, the hinge in the door
to the underworld,

the moon, a mouth of a saxophone,
    sexy and malignant.

It was midnight, Jesus
    about to be born again
for the nineteen-hundred-and-eighty-fifth time.

Red and green lights blinked
    like heart monitors. I fell asleep
between migrations, the heron just arriving.

Great horned owls built nests
    of grasses and clay.

Inside their custard wombs, bones
    were churning. When I woke,
nurses appeared, vespers

from the snowdrifts of Christmas
    brought into a room the world boxed up
with heavy postage, ready to be shipped off.

I woke into a little doorstep of the day,
    the frame of my house under construction
where I kept you safe behind my ribs.

Already, the kingfishers were headed
    into Mexico, guided by the inner compass
we have no answers for.

Sonogram

Blood hums
    in the halls and holy rooms
of the heart.

Pearl, fetus, little prophet,
    by now transformed from cartilage
to bone,

bearing eyebrows and fingernails,
    sucking your thumb in a sheath of creamy vernix,
listening with cochlear intaglio

inside this preface, sound tide,
    acoustic wand of frequency, red shift to blue,
imaging depth of field, uncertainty.

With me on this gurney, shroud
    of intensive care, you burn
in an amniotic lake, nerves flashing,

coated with myelin,
    hair and milk-teeth buds sprouting.
Echolations of anatomy—

umbilical—swishing. Rope.
    Conduit to the new world.

The final image: your hand, opening
    and closing like a blossom

three times—

I am alive, I am alive.
    I am.

The Flower-Crowned Skull of Saint Valentine

We discover the skull in the reliquary
belonged to the patron saint of epilepsy,

beheaded after assisting persecuted martyrs.
Often painted with red roses and a rooster,

he performs a wedding, bears a sword,
and holds the sun, giving sight to a blind girl.

On the scans, my brain appears
like a galaxy—planets, comets,

veins, arteries. More information here
than in the historic heart. Logic *and* passion.

Memory fields, black holes of loss, cognition,
the central nervous system wired to send

messages, like the love letter I write to you
tucked in the envelope of the parietal lobe.

I think of this as I enter my third year
without seizures, electrical disturbances

of the temporal quadrant, dormant for now
as we mail our valentines, step into the boat,

row toward the future, slip a wreath,
bramble of thorns, into water.

Day Two

I feed him milk, oxygen, sunlight.

Crickets play their flutes,
tiny as eyelashes,

green shoulder blades tuck back
into a trapezoidal dignity.

A geometry of trillium glows in the dark.
On his blanket, wings of swans

folded elegant and diaphanous.
I am transported by this division of cells,

followed by his eyes
before we know their color.

Sharm El Sheikh

Darling, when I think of how we nearly went to Sharm
El Sheikh, plotting the trip, unfolding the crinkled maps
in bed, it's as if we really did go on that journey.
After the pyramids, of course, where you held me against
the cool stone wall, entombed with kings and queens
dead for four thousand years. And how then we entered
the waters off Sharm El Sheikh, an envelope of blue,
so warm I swam the backstroke out to sea. Remember
the anemones and clown fish, the waves causing them
to sway back and forth in the current? And the moon
jellyfish that stung so, I spent the rest of the day swollen
in bed? And then the bombing. And how everything closed
and no one swam. No food or fresh water. No flights.
Let's don't go back to that place we never left for.
Let's look at the maps on our bodies at home.
Let's pull up the comforter and travel again.

Yellowtail

The war was over.
We sutured the wounded,

buried the dead, sat at the bar
with the enemy near the blue

throat of the sea. A sushi chef
slivered salmon into orchids,

etched clouds from oysters,
as they rose snowing pearls.

From shrimp and seaweed
he shaped hummingbirds

that hovered above us.
With the world's smallest blade

he carved from yellowfin
miniature flanks of horses.

They cantered around our hands.

Girl with a Pearl Earring, Vermeer

I was looking for *The Goldfinch*
but saw her first.

I stared back at her.
We had this conversation.

I could feel her breath
and body heat, the scent of lye soap,

but hadn't I seen her the week before
at the market in Delft

touching yellow apples?
Wasn't she wearing that same dress

but bloodstained?
I had tried to get her attention,

and though she turned to me with that look
she disappeared past the meat market.

And hadn't I seen her in D.C.
on 14th and V, in the soup kitchen?

At the rape crisis center in Santa Fe?
In my grandmother who could not report it?

If I'd known where to find her
I would have spoken

but she's in the newspaper every day,
or taking her children

to school, keeping secrets, sleeping
on OxyContin.

Girl Reading a Letter, Vermeer

In the window of wavy glass, her face—
milky, trapped there—a phantom on a boat
stealing sailors from whales and drowning.

On the edge of shadow, a bowl of fruit
toppled over, uneaten,
a breakfast from her worried mother.

Birdsong dives in, knits a small nest
beneath the navel. Here is the bed,
a blood-red tapestry, woven

into a geometry of villages,
crumpled just as the night he mounted her
like a swan, told the story, called her Leda.

Her bodice is loosened.
Her breasts heave.
She reads—

Boy

I read to the boy, a knight, king, captain
of a ship, Robin Hood stealing alms
from my purse at midnight.

The dusty black dog breathes bear-heavy.
Pockets in jeans fill with boy treasure—

    sliver of bone, mica,
    empty diamond skin of snake,
    feathers, blue velvet of fallen grackle.

He speaks to doves in the field.
They coo, and by the evening candle
the Manx cat purrs from his cradled hands
the way a lion will in the arms of Daniel.

The Ear Is a Bony Labyrinth

The child eventually grows into his.
They bend, sail, unfurl, twin nests attached

so close to the bone of his cheek,
lobes suspended in mid-air

just at the early road of his neck.
They jut for a song from each

choir to enter the head, scribe
into memory. Primary vessels

bear the murmur of lexicon,
mysterious and lush,

like letters inside their envelopes
waiting to be read.

Acupuncture with Dr. Hao

There are ninety-seven points on the ear.

Three women on the bank sip tea
from celadon cups.

A quartet plays something exquisite.

He takes my pulse as though searching
a map for a forbidden city,

reaches through hidden meridians

in the landscape of this interior.
He thinks *spleen, lung.*

I am in Guangzhou.

The Pearl River opens beyond
the emerald bamboo forest.

Dr. Hao navigates a boat within
the channel of immortals,

dips his oars into water, rows
toward the future for a cure.

Dr. Suto's Herbs

Insomniacs. It's this relationship with the moon,
an ability to sense touch behind walls,

the third eye keeping vigil for the sick,
surveillance for a cure.

He listens to my pulse: gaunt whisper,
skitter of a nocturnal creature,

performs with needles—beautiful daggers,
long dashes in a Dickinson poem.

There are herbs to take: hooves of cattle
during the Year of the Ox,

chrysanthemum powder, scales of golden
koi, wet ash of a cremated geisha—

Drink, and you shall become very small.
And I do—disappear in the chorus of alert,

fall from the rim of awake, echo
down the tunnel of subconscious—

visitation rights with the unborn,
conversations with the dead,

a terror of flaws and an emperor's
fortune of happiness, the intuitive eye

reversing direction behind its lid.
I float. I sleep. Dreams undulate

into the sound of a thousand
paper parasols opening

before a storm
on Shijo Street.

Atlas

Where I travel, anise in the Pernod
    tastes of yellow silk.

My body, buoyant on the surface
    of water. Underneath,

a mute conversation of fish.
    Waterfalls gush against

the cloud's texture,
    ions with a fluid text of answers.

A long stand of palm trees,
    footprints from space.

Verdant mountains camouflage
    a pyramid the way skin

covers anatomy: the X-ray of *I am*
    stripped to stiff, wobbly film,

skull above crossbones—
    piracy, poison.

The horizon is empty
    but for a hunter's moon.

The elk mate all night.

Moustafa

Moustafa lights a rock veined with sparkles.
Frankincense. His passion for ancient scents.

In his apothecary of jars filled with minerals
and powders, salves line the shelves.

This, for insomnia—oil of orange blossoms,
he passes under our nostrils.

And here, for snoring. No more night music,
as he dips the oil on a rag, passing it to us.

I note eucalyptus. I know later
my husband will attempt a lecture

about the possibility of catching
a rare disease from this.

And here, argan oil to ensure you live long, my friend,
or drizzle over eggplant with seven-spice tagine.

I take a mixture for fish, an infusion for the liver,
cardamom for digestion, amber for moths,

a root for asthma, but on the way out I see
jars of flower buds, bones, a bird

wing, amulets for seizures.
I want to know everything.

After the Diagnosis

We walked to the pond, considered the swans'
question-mark necks wet with bite marks, listened
to the honking of snow geese mating for life.

I visited the museum with its displays of oddities:
foreign objects fished out of children—
shiny pins, sharp nails, clips and thorns

retrieved by the precision of a surgeon's hands.
The evolution of medicine—what was once
so painful, personal—now given a label

displayed on cadavers. That night there was a man
in the restaurant whose arm shot up involuntarily,
as if raising his hand to answer. Strangers,

we spoke among ourselves about vials of blood
the techs had drawn all week, tubes of crimson cells,
our grasping of appointment cards, the weekly

epistle we memorized for hours in waiting rooms,
as if to audition for a longer life. At St. Mary's
Hospital, they threaded an artery in the groin,

a catheter to deliver dye.
The beautiful photographs of my brain
I keep now in the drawer beneath my hats—

an angiogram of my skull,
its shadows and clustered veins,
teeth lined up in their ghostly corridors.

Everything becomes inquisitive now,
aside from the heart—transparent and rhythmic

with all of its defects,
its innocent murmur knowing nothing.

A Love Supreme

—John Coltrane

No coincidence that in Renaissance paintings
the angels play horns.

They had that right. It's about the resurrection
one comes into after so much suffering—

digging in, spinning a hymn without words,
the evolution of his song—

the Angelus, *Acknowledgment* (I have
wronged), how love turns itself on

finding *Resolution* in the greater Master—
the one who saves you (from yourself),

Pursuance of this crepuscular heaven,
passages in *Psalms*—notes

translated through a horn—
a deep flower, blue throat of joy.

St. Vincent Infirmary

In the house of illness they harvest pain
for the master of misery, while seraphs sing

about fluids of the body, chant the Gospel
of Suffering in their muffled voices.

I imagine them on rooftop gardens—
figures in air moving through red geraniums,

ministering to the sick. Here, blood
drools sinister and biblical, amber

secretions, froth of infection.
In the traffic of needles, a stone path

leads through ancient columns of the spine:
lumbar, thorax, cervical. At night,

a dark field of mustard, at midnight,
the back side of a dream in the drifts of snow.

Each brick, set by a mason
to build the mansion of sleep in a drip.

At the end of a long hall, a red neon
sunset announces, Exit.

There is no other way to escape,
unless you see the light

before the finish line in the brain,
like dusk on the garden at home

where your child holds a peach,
transports the scent

of orchards in sunlight,
hundreds of birds collecting

in the air, all blue at the gate
of your pale, porous body.

Organ Donor

Take this estate of my body.

Steal my eyes, black pearls, prisms
for an audience weary of rain.

Wear my heart, love, lungs to fill
the hollow. Let my skull

be a nest for the nuthatch,
a music box for the passerby.

Take what you seek
and let me disappear.

I will be the ghost, a rind
in the company of fruit.

Living with the Dead

We try to bring them back

in ritual, chant, narrative, legend,
promising theories that never deliver.

I build altars, light candles
beneath daguerreotypes,

hold them in dreams
where their skin is warm.

We invite them to join us,
though they have moved on,

rowed their boats, gold and powerful,
over the edge of the horizon.

Baggage, Prophet

She tells me to bring my troubles
soon after the large piñon in back bleeds sap,
a sticky death, its weeping glued to the trunk.
I take out the scratched leather suitcase
with the straps and the sticker of the state of Wyoming,
gather the thirteen-year-old boy in, his eyes that shoot
St. Sebastian darts. I thought if Jane were packing
she would deposit her beautiful lost breasts
like ghost limbs. I bag the stormy stomach,
the disturbing yellow wasps that cling to the lining.
The mystic, she empties the valise, secretly refills it.
I open, see the boy with eyes of Gabriel,
a field of wild flowers
back in his body and a note to say
fear will suck the holy grit from you,
banish you to a strange country
where no one speaks your language.

II

Widow Fetish

There are no charms left to bring me back—

no more bones and straw, shells and dung,
red threads with blood honey.

The bend in the stream is the wolf I wrestle with.

A million silver fins we cleaned, gutted,
swim by in my sleep.

Didn't we eat them?
Wasn't the water clean?

Don't punish me any longer
with what shivers.

Disappearing into water at the end of the day
with her dress on, a girl

melts below the skin of a lake.

Union

He breathes the same rhythm in your sleep.
She is present in the ashes of loneliness.

You pray to him bead by bead,
rest your weary head on his leg of kindness.

She blesses you with crops,
sets moons in the sky to plant by.

You burn sage, measure
the world next to her waist.

She feeds you oranges from Singapore,
nut meats from Tangier.

Does she wear trees or rubies?
Does he wear war?

You bring her tuberose and lilacs.
Wait for him between the shift of clouds.

Of the Holy Ghost

When my father arrives at the door of my dreams
he comes from the wing-lidded coffin where I saw him last,

his sons and daughters crouched around his body,
Apostles at the Last Supper.

Father of the Holy Ghost.
Of memory and the daily bread.

He told me once: *If ever off course*

follow the stream from the mountain to a river
then a lake, toward lights. It will keep you alive.

Most days I prefer to be lost
in the switchbacks of forgotten trails.

When my father appears, his eyes are Chartres blue.
He has been weeping. His voice,

not unlike the martyr constantly flogged.
I open the door wider. I let my father in.

Sightings from the Hungry Ghost Camp

When I wake from the nightmare,
I know someone familiar has opened

all the creaking doors to the windy subconscious,
entered the treble clef of the coral brain.

Now I see it is you again, ghost. In dreams
you curl your finger, a snail from its shell,

signal to come closer. Owls peer in.
Espíritu, Pax Domini, beehive of a spirit home.

Yet this week, with the moon parked
in its new house, you sit behind empty bottles,

reaching your hands out, which is everything,
the *floating world,* space above flame and flood.

Addiction

That was the house we built
around ourselves

sealing all the doors
and windows before

swallowing
the key.

Triad for the Body

1. Self

Written in shadow—X-rays dipped through the light.
Footnotes of organs plotted by nuclear medicine.

2. Illness

The oncologist says the tumor possesses hair and teeth.
What is it? he asks.

Names it: my little friend.
Nights, he calls it: *Enemy. Intelligentsia.*

The mutation breaks into the body of his home
through seven sacred openings—

its heat ducts and sockets, vestibule
and transept, mouth of a chalice.

Mephisto stalks by the night window
steals his food, burns the field.

I find him disappearing in the vast countryside
of his bed but for two blue ocean eyes

and the oxygen tank,
a whispering lung.

I will fear no evil.

3. Cadaver

Sketching impressions
in a notebook of mirror writing,

da Vinci secretly examined them
by six candles through the night.

Vespers

When she leaves her body
she disappears to a lake
the color of glaciers,
slips through the lip of water,
swims inside a tabernacle.

All that is chronic disappears:
desire, cancer, ache, hunger.
I search the globes of her fixed pupils
and think: witness, birth of a child,
death of a mother.

Someone closes her eyelids.
We step away from the breeze.

On Each Horizon at Dusk

There is a house of night: tenants of dreams,
ghosts, a white kimono, speech lowered
to a whisper. It's as if what we carry

becomes lighter—egg to feather, lightning
to the gossamer of rain, a corner of loneliness
to a room for tenderness—

each sound, soft as a kiss or breath,
the distant ocean from a shell or wind,
just before it catches, taking hold in a sail.

Photographer of War, Sebastião Salgado

Behind the aperture of his retina
I see how sweat floods

across the landscape of bodies
stripped of shirts and dresses.

Gazing from tall ladders, leaning in
to faces with skin of thin paper lanterns

and torsos spare
as the tongues of prophets.

Peripatetic, eternally in danger,
he traps human shadow

with his magic box
now in possession of a soul.

Anatomy

To draw the human figure,
da Vinci secretly dissected cadavers—

wrists steeped in viscera,
knuckles knocking bones.

He must have known his rival,
Michelangelo, engaged in forbidden

autopsies as well, devoted to a worker's
muscle, a child's organ, the eye's hinge.

Discovered the mandible, horseshoe
of the jaw, which opens while speaking,

and tracked the cochlea of the inner ear,
a rising serpent coiled inside the skull.

Throughout the body—sinew, pulse
of river-blue veins. Heaven

and science, a complex math.
The skin, cover of a holy text.

After Each Act of Grief

Close the ethereal body down.
Place it in a tomb
or burn it.

When we're born again, small
windows above the ear appear
where goldfinch sing.

Where a porthole through the cranium
unbolts into lilacs

over the walls of heaven.
Everything answers.

Even this acequia, trickling
through the desert, suddenly
becomes the Ganges

spilling holy water
from the mountain.

His fragrance, the breeze.
Her touch, the grasses.

Everything answers.

Fellini's *Roma*

Beneath the subway, the newly discovered
prehistoric cave: red bison, five handprints.

Within minutes the pigment fades, then dissolves
from the sudden burst of air. Federico wears
a miner's hat, dirt, khakis, and boots. Darkness

surrounds him. He is thinking fragment, delicate,
the world of primitive and new, his mother's Vespa,
a modern chariot. It happens to be Ash Wednesday

and he considers the Archbishop's liturgy
at the Vatican, from dust to dust. He senses
catacombs, the beds of bones, of earth and salt,

Mussolini, and the eternal city. Fellini slides against
the wall of rock in the cool, once-sealed cavern,
sits on the most ancient dirt of his country

while he imagines bordellos, Puccini,
a baritone coming down the aisle
the way a storm enters a parched valley.

He reflects on Mass, the confessional, three boxes—
forgiveness in the middle of the two sides of sin.
The taste of Chianti, fusilli, the way cypresses grow

in long neat rows along the road to San Pellegrino.
The lace of his wife's black mantilla,
of weight and measure, the way water fills

in arched aqueducts, their scheduled holes,
the ancient history in his blood moaning
among the ruins, a sound that will carry

forever in his genes, a certain frantic attachment
through the instantaneous separation
of the departed from being.

Train to Rome

I was twenty-two, a passenger in a box car
bearing down the tracks. I chewed black cherries,
rewrote the seven deadly sins, applied Pomodoro
lipstick, drank grappa. I wore red stilettos
and don't remember the details, but I smoldered
off that train, drifted into the Vatican, past the Bernini
doors, Fra Angelicos, and Giotto's tryptych—
inside the wing of the *Pietà*, spellbound
by marble bodies, mother and son in the light,
visceral, veins beneath their flesh of stone.
The arch of his neck in the nest of her arm.
How resigned she was to grief and how my life
was not, not yet. A large crowd had gathered.
It seemed prophets hunkered among us.
I peered into the cracked door of the future,
and saw sorrow and its fierce latitudes.

Szymborska

Some of her books I keep
in the drawer near my bed.

Should I open a hotel
all the night stands will embrace her.

And I would place lavender there
and vials of tears

to invoke dreams of purple fields
in Poland during spring,

and little crosses like warplanes
in their hangars put to rest.

Astrology, the Reading

Nearly all planets are aligned, redefined,
although Mercury is retrograde. Again.

Fate. Statistics say this happens in the land
of beauty and inefficiency

at least five days out of each month.
It bleeds. We cry. Life is short.

Question dark angels
having to negate your passion.

He tells you not to wear lipstick?
Wear the brightest red vermilion.

He's tired? Dance anyway.
However, by the middle of the week

when Virgo and Mars trine with the sun
and the third house is on Leo,

when the galaxies mix their potion
of jealousy, do not run.

Make him surrender
to the tongues of wet flowers,

lick the tears from every eye.
Jupiter looms large above your house.

(He will claim that it is he, his planet.
Do not believe him.)

There is nothing to forgive
or to be made any better than this—

his hands as large as stars,
his breath—clouds sailing above the moon.

There is no sin, no stain, only joy, red pears,
love juice, watermelon, and a fish turned golden

on the grill. A glass of water. Two lemons.
The Kronos Quartet

playing something strangely madrigal.
Life is a dog. Run with it.

Frida Kahlo, *Self-Portrait with Thorn Necklace and Hummingbird*

At the party on Day of the Dead, a table spills over
with marigold, pomegranates, votive candles, a life-sized,
white chocolate skeleton that we cannibals feast on
as though on our own bodies. The spine climbs
into the ivory patina skull—one's kingdom—filled
with scripture, echo of Chronos. The teeth, a harmonica
of bone glints. Eye sockets, two deep wells for field mice.

In a corner, ghouls and witches smoke cigarettes.
Dead brides read horoscopes, steal futures.
The historical rise from their coffins. Penelope of Ithaca
and Nero from Rome. There is a man who never slept
and a woman named Zero. Sisters of vampires and a priest
give a eulogy on *la vida*. Seek your ancestors from the family
album and ghosts will whisper from their photos.

So many Frida Kahlos and Diego Riveras, so many
that I wonder if there is a look-alike contest for the two
artists from Mexico City. And there is. All those women
sport knitted brows and mustaches. Their hair, sculptures
of braids, knotted ornaments. They wear long, colorful
skirts, peasant blouses embroidered with crimson hibiscus,
but not to disguise disfigurement. Or embarrassment.

No one wears a necklace of thorns and hummingbird.
No monkey rides the shoulder through the jungle
of suffering. No one here born in La Casa Azul,
stricken with polio, born with spina bifida,
spina diablo, spine of the devil.

Back then, time was told by a rooster under a tree full of mangos.
In *medianoche* the sky surrenders the moon like an eye,
through the window, closer. Pain does this—burns you
through nightfall as you lie cursing the teeth of stars.

Milagros

Each year I buy a *milagro*—
a small silver amulet, *ex-voto*.

A horse, then a heart. A house
and a bird. A tiny green Buddha

and a dog that looks just like yours,
the one who stayed with you

when you were four, lost
in the maze of arroyos, then found.

How strange in this techno world,
the X-rays of you inside

and outside of me, the miracle
of diagnosis and survival,

how in the book of grace, two figures
turned to three, each of us alive.

The way you became bone,
flesh, blood, teeth—divine.

Searching for God through the Medina After Dark

After the oud players have infused you
with rapture—

turn left at the red threads of saffron,
right at fresh mint,

one-half kilometer through the burning
of frankincense.

Don't breathe too deeply
through the scent of turning meat

until, in the open air
of coffee shops and taxis,

a man offers you a ride
to a camel in the desert

where you find yourself
under the host of a full moon

in the sign of Cancer,
listening to the faint hum

of the last call
to prayer.

Flight 387

Today is a plane occupied
by Moroccans and Italians.

Some believe in Mohammed,
others pray to Jesus.

Some wear a hijab,
a few are in jeans.

The plane ascends through turbulence
until it levels at 30,000 feet.

All are served coffee or tea.
An attendant delivers menus

with a footnote that says,
does not contain pork.

There is pasta with cheese
and tagine with dates and chicken.

A mother speaks Berber.
A father, a dialect from Sardinia:

My child needs water.
May I have a blanket?

I am still hungry.
When all have eaten

and the sky darkens,
a baby cries out, then another.

It's as if they understand
each other.

Tonight, all will cross an ocean.
Tomorrow, a border.

In the Center of Night, the Heart Slips
Out of Its Socket

builds a nest in the solar plexus,
squirms there.

Now and then it dresses up,
ventures out, dances

to the music of vespers
and Latin guitars, or murmurs

with water under a bridge
in an ancient Chinese painting.

Sometimes there's arrhythmia,
that erratic short circuit of loneliness,

but tonight the heart is an organ of joy,
of love's circulation, valves opening

for tiny boats of happiness.

Invocation

When your altar is lit
with a sea of candles

think of me,
your impure thoughts turned holy.

Search for me
like Odysseus finding his way back home

past deafening Sirens,
baiting temptresses, and the one-eyed cyclops.

Trust me.
Open me like a prayer book

where I sing Hymn No. 49
Angels Brush Us with Great Gray Wings.

Lucy

The skull, a locket
of scripture, data,

scaffolding for the face.

The pelvis, a cradle,
future.

Mother, now that my son
has rivered into a man,

I rock you.
I hold you

up.

Fidelity

No more messages in amber or celadon bottles,
or letters full of bees

smoked out of glued envelopes, stamped
with gargoyles from your corner of hell.

Oui, you are the navigator of this small boat.
Yes, the silver needle on the compass points true north.

Non, the sun is not temporary.
Oui, the moon is a mountainous eye with a vision.

Look, already you are asleep
inside the body of the mother

in your dreams.
Yes, you will be delivered.

Notes

The Goldfinch is a painting by Carel Fabritius. This, and "The Girl with a Pearl Earring," are housed in the Mauritshius Museum in Holland.

"Cerebral Hemorrhage, Five Months with Child, Christmas Eve" refers to a brain hemorrhage I experienced the night before Christmas at five months pregnant.

The flower-crowned skull of St. Valentine resides in the Basilica of Santa Maria in Cosmedin, Rome.

Sharm El Sheikh is an Egyptian town between the desert of the Sinai Peninsula and the Red Sea, known for its clear waters and coral reefs.

"Floating world" (*ukiyo*) describes an era during Japan's Edo period (1615–1868) and evokes an imaginary universe of style and extravagance, hedonism and transgression—the opposite of everyday obligation.

"Drink and you shall become very small" refers to a line in Lewis Carroll's *Alice's Adventures in Wonderland*.

"Photographer of War" refers to Brazilian photographer Sebastião Salgado.

Fusilli is a corkscrew-shaped pasta.

Pernod is an anise-flavored apéritif from France.

Lucy refers to the early (3.2 million years ago) female hominid discovered in Ethiopia.

In the poem, "Frida Kahlo. . ." Chronos is the personification of time in pre-Socratic philosophy.

Milagros is the Spanish word for miracles and for amulets representing different parts of the body.

An *ex-voto* is a votive offering to a saint or to a divinity.

A Love Supreme, by John Coltrane, is a suite in four parts: "Acknowledgement," "Resolution," "Pursuance," and "Psalm."

"Fellini's *Roma*" refers to Federico Fellini's 1972 film.

The poem "Invocation" refers to Sirens, from Greek mythology, who were dangerous female creatures, partly human, known to lure nearby sailors with their music, causing them to shipwreck.

In "Triad for the Body," the italicized line is from Psalm 23.

"Szymborska" refers to Wislawa Szymborska (1923–2012), the Polish poet who received the Nobel Prize in Literature in 1996.

Acknowledgments

Grateful acknowledgment to the places where these poems first appeared, sometimes in slightly different versions or differently titled:

The American Journal of Poetry: "Train to Rome," "Sharm El Sheikh," and "Triad for the Body"
Audible Fire (anthology): "Atlas" and "Photographer of War"
Baltimore Review: "A Love Supreme"
Blue Mesa Review: "On Each Horizon at Dusk" and "The Ear Is a Bony Labyrinth"
Borderlands: "Szymborska"
Boulevard: "Girl with a Pearl Earring, Vermeer"
The Columbia Review: "Widow Fetish"
Cortland Review: "After the Diagnosis"
Hawaii Pacific Review: "The Flower-Crowned Skull of St. Valentine"
Indiana Review: "Dr. Soto's Herbs"
Innisfree: "Boy," "Milagros," and "Roma"
Massachusetts Review: "Vespers"
New Mexico Discovery (anthology): "Union," "Day Two," and "Astrology"
Nimrod: "Anatomy"
Oranges & Sardines: "Madonna with Child, Christmas Eve" and "St. Vincent's Infirmary (Hotel Pain)"
Poemeleon: "Girl Reading a Letter, Vermeer" and "Sonogram"
Poet Lore: "Acupuncture with Dr. Hao"
Poetry: "Yellowtail"
Prairie Schooner: "Leave the Barren Fields"
Santa Fe Writer's Project: "Frida Kahlo, *Self-Portrait with Thorn Necklace*"
Santa Fe Literary Review: "Hymn"
Southern Humanities Review: "Lucy"
Tinderbox: "Fidelity"
Windmill, Oklahoma University: "Baggage"

"Photographer of War" was republished in *THE Magazine*, and was selected by Sam Hamill for "Poets Against the War," an article in *The Monthly Review*.

"Madonna with Child, Christmas Eve" was selected for the Rita Dove Award.

Thanks to Grace Cavalieri, Ken Flynn, and the Library of Congress' podcast program of readings and interviews, *The Poet and the Poem*, on which readings of some of these poems have appeared. They can be heard under "Holly Bass and Mary Morris" at the Library of Congress website: www.loc.gov.

Special thanks to my parents, Thomas and Frances Morris; my son, Daniel DeVito: my husband, Ken Apt; John DeVito; Caren Reed Smith; Lauren and Jon Fidge; and Cathy and Kent Hanson.

Thanks to X.J. Kennedy for selecting this manuscript for publication.

Immense appreciation to the people who gave invaluable feedback on this manuscript through its various stages: Ioanna Carlsen, Maggie Smith, Thomas Centolella, and Dana Levin.

Much gratitude to my poety group who made suggestions for many of these poems as early drafts: Gary Worth Moody, Barbara Rockman, Donald Levering, Robyn Covelli Hunt, Debby Casillas, Anne Haven McDonnell, and Kim Parko.

Gracias for all the sparks, Joan Logghe. Thanks to Tony Hoagland for his community classes and to Richard Lehnert for his finely-tuned copy editing.

Special thanks to Kim Davis and her staff at Texas Review Press, a member of Texas A&M University Press Consortium, TAMU.

About the Author

Mary Morris received the Rita Dove Award and the New Mexico Discovery Award. Published in *Poetry, Prairie Schooner, The Columbia Review, Arts & Letters,* and numerous other literary journals, she has been invited to read at the Library of Congress and consequently aired on NPR. She lives in Santa Fe, New Mexico.

CPSIA information can be obtained
at www.ICGtesting.com
Printed in the USA
LVOW03s0804160318
570043LV00001BA/9/P